Summary of

Catch and Kill: Lies, Spies and a Conspiracy to Protect Predators

By Ronan Farrow

Goodbooks

Summary of Catch and Kill: Lies, Spies and a Conspiracy to Protect Predators By Ronan Farrow Published by Books, Inc, 8 The Green, Suite R, Dover, County of Kent, 19901, Delaware

https://books.inc/

© 2020 Books, Inc

CONTENTS

Overview

Catch and Kill: Lies, Spies, and a Conspiracy to Protect Predators is a homage to good, old-fashioned reporting. Written by Ronan Farrow, he shares the challenges he struggled with chasing Harvey Weinstein's many years of the alleged rape, sexual abuse and sexual harassment of women. The 'catch and kill' is a media covert technique in which media companies catch, buy and bury negative stories. Farrow's journalism followed the truth and exposed Weinstein's practices, despite many hurdles.

He narrates the stories of numerous women who suffered because of Weinstein's abuse with heart-touching details, aiming to bring into the spotlight the hardships of an industry ruled by money, power, and abuse. He tracks his efforts against Weinstein's efforts to 'catch and kill' the story, which is peppered with disturbing narratives of harassment and cowardice or collusion of media outlets. When NBC refuses to pursue and publish his story, New York Times accepts it, which won Farrow a Pulitzer Prize.

Harvey Weinstein's company was aware of his bullying behavior and kept funds for addressing his "sexual harassment" and "physical abuse"

Ronan Farrow narrates how winners at many film and television award ceremonies often thanked producer Harvey Weinstein for his exquisite input. Weinstein was popular for the success and power he held within the film industry. But the truth is that: *"Weinstein wheedled and menaced and bullied and didn't take no for an answer."* Farrow commences his narration by setting the stage and the roots of Weinstein's money and power. Harvey Weinstein and his brother Bob launched Miramax, a film production studio launched by Harvey and his brother Bob in memory of their parents, Miriam and Max. The company was bought by Disney in the early 1990s and in the 2000s, the two brothers raised millions when the relationship finalized. They used the funds to launch the Weinstein Company. Some of their best, Oscar-winning movies include *The Artist* released in 2011 and *The King's Speech* in 2010.

Farrow, the narrator, asserts that Miramax used to maintain funds in order to cover Weinstein's bullying, harassment, and abuse of money. The funds were used by the former president of the marketing department Dennis Rice to compensate women and make them remain quiet by threatening their careers. Sixteen former and current employees acknowledged these practices. Fabrizio Lombardo's main job was to lead Miramax Italy, but many saw his main job as 'recruiting' women for his boss, although he denied it. Farrow states that he was "essentially a pimp on company roll". The thin job description was used as a cover-up for his primary role of getting women to their boss. The women he procured used to go with Weinstein to meetings where they used to leave him with other women only to be victimized. Emily Nestor told Farrow that, back in 2014, Weinstein invited her for a few drinks, while she was a front desk attendant at Miramax. He offered to help her advance her career, suggesting that she should become his girlfriend. He continued his harassment towards Emily Nestor by pursuing her aggressively in the workplace and trying to convince her to go to his hotel room. When Nestor attempted to contact HR, she was informed that all complaints will be disclosed to him. This policy, along with many others at his company, kept Weinstein's victims away from filing formal complaints that would damage his reputations. This is one of his many acts on keeping his victim silent.

Weinstein was a long-term target for reporters

During reporting a story regarding the Hollywood casting couch, Farrow's boss, Noah Oppenheim, suggests him to contact Rose McGowan, an actress who identified herself as being Weinstein's rape victim. McGowan was writing a book, aiming to expose Weinstein, but she considered speaking in front of a live camera. When she considered speaking the truth in from of the camera, a lawyer told her that no one would believe her because she'd performed simulated sex scenes in movies and her claims against a studio head would be untrustworthy and eventually futile.

Although many reporters pursued Weinstein's harassment stories, none of them were successful, although much evidence indicated towards his partake in such acts. He spent his time and efforts to discover people who are willing to defend Weinstein but to no avail. Donna Gigliotti, who is the producer of *Shakespeare in Love,* mentioned to Farrow that other reports spent their time and resources trying to uncover Weinstein's abusive practices, too, without any palpable results.

One of the reporters who sought to uncover the truth was Ken Auletta, who knew two women in Miramax London who settled a joint sexual harassment case. Both women received Weinstein's personal check, but he denied the story and Auletta ended up refocusing his article on his aggressive behaviors. On a similar note, New York Magazine's writer Ben Wallace made more efforts to pursue the same story. Weinstein's people seem to know that we worked for the New York Times, thus the magazine decided that it is not worth it to suffer Weinstein's revengeful behavior.

Actress Rose McGowen eventually lost her contract with Amazon Studios after she told the studio that she was Weinstein's rape victim. McGowen shared with Farrow that she believed that someone was following her; eventually, a private detective informed Farrow that his investigation of Weinstein's behaviors triggered his surveillance, too.

Nine women were further assaulted or abused by Weinstein

In 2015, model Ambra Gutierrez contacted the police and wore a wire at the next meeting with Weinstein, where he freely discusses his aggressive behaviors. Although the police believed her, the District Attorney Cyrus Vance Jr.'s office suddenly dropped the case, even though in the past he pursued cases with much less evidence. Farrow highlights that Weinstein made a series of hefty donations to political parties, which supported Vance's re-election. The media shamed Gutierrez, claiming she was a prostitute, and her lawyers convinced her to settle.

Furthermore, Annabella Sciorra narrates how Weinstein follower her to her home, although not at first. Weinstein entered her apartment forcefully, pushed her on the bed and raped her. She did not go to the police or fight Weinstein, but her career still met its end; the rumors were that she is a bit difficult and she did not find any work for three years, from 1992 to 1995. In 1997, she participated in the Cannes Film Festival, where Weinstein appeared at her hotel room door, with a bottle of baby oil. Sciorra desperately ran to the phone, pushing buttons in madness. When the hotel staff arrived, Weinstein left. At the same Cannes festival, he approached actress Daryl Hannah. He aggressively banged at her hotel room until she ran away through the back door. The following day, he repeated his behavior, and she blocked the door with pieces of furniture. Years later, he got access to her room in Rome and, seeing her makeup artist was present, he claimed that she is needed at the party downstairs. When she arrived, the room was empty and Weinstein demanded to touch her breasts. When she mentioned the incident, no one took her seriously and the event remained undealt with.

Farrow further reports Ashely Judd's story, who also implied that Weinstein harassed her sexually, but never mentioned his name. Rosanna Arquette, a fellow actress, went to Weinstein's room, where he only had a bathrobe on. He requested a neck massage and when she pulled back, he gripped her hand, forcing her towards his erection. Weinstein told her refusing him was a mistake; later, her career also met an early end.

Some women agreed to long-term relationships with Weinstein out of fear

Although contradictory, some women had purely humane responses to his behaviors. Asia Argento, an Italian actress, was brought by Lombardo to Weinstein's room. When Weinstein returned from the bathroom, he was dressed in a bathrobe and requested a massage. Argento was intimidated and she agreed, but Weinstein forced her skirt up and legs apart. Argento felt guilty for many years that she did not stop him. In addition to this, they also had other sexual happenstances. However, she never fought him due to his involvement in her professional life and the fear of what might happen: the early end to a career that many other women previously experienced.

Weinstein's victims were chased off with The National Enquirer's negative stories

The book's title comes to light once Farrow explains the practices of National Enquirer and how Weinstein managed to remain away from the spotlights with his numerous acts of sexual abuse and harassment. American Media (AMI) is the owner of *The National Enquirer,* an establishment that sought to pursue negative stories about anyone who accused Weinstein in an attempt to "catch and kill". Farrow unearthed how AMI caught and killed stories about Sylvester Stallone, Arnold Schwarzenegger, and Donald Trump. They used to grab accusers' medical records and publish negative stories located at the edge of the law. This practice is often employed by media outlets, which discover and buy stories about influential people with the purpose of burying them.

Farrow discovered more concerning information about the Enquirer's internal practices. Although they kept safe any information they discovered and did not use, editor-in-chief Dylon Howard ordered his employees in 2016 to shred all the papers kept in a safe concerning Donald Trump. Later, he refused to acknowledge this act. Associated Press exposed the company's CEO misbehaviors, claiming that he made his employees watch porn films and made comments on the female employees' intimate lives.

How Weinstein collected information about his accusers

Farrow reports that Weinstein hired K2 Intelligence to pursue investigations on Ambra Gutierrez. When she decided to file a claim against him regarding his harassment acts, he shared the findings with New York's district attorney. He then retained the NSO Group, a company which is known for their Pegasus software. The group can control cellphones and extract private data. Farrow was also informed that the private investigative firm PSOPS used to investigate him and share the information with Weinstein.

Furthermore, Black Cube was hired by Weinstein, a company whose operatives used false identities to survey their targets. Black Cube hired 'Anna', a woman who befriended McGowan and gain access to the book she was writing about her experience with Weinstein.

Black Cube also investigated Farrow while its arrangement with Weinstein. Farrow acquired most of his information from an anonymous source, Sleeper1973, who shared emails and contracts with him. Farrow was spied by Igor Ostrovskiy and other subcontractors of Black Cube.

Igor Ostrovskiy approached him when the information he was leaking became too uncomfortable. In Ostrovskiy's homeland, the oppression of journalists was a common practice; he refused to accept a similar situation in the United States and told Farrow the truth. This is how Farrow managed to shed light on the labyrinth of corruption.

First failed attempts at publishing the report

Noah Oppenheim, the president of NBC News; Andy Lack, his boss running NBC News and MSNBC; Steve Burke as NBC Universal's CEO; Brian Roberts as NBC's parent company Comcast CEO. They all have in common one behavior: telling Farrow to stop his investigation on Weinstein at some point during it. NBC executives were asked by Weinstein about his endeavors and he was assured that he will not publish the reported while he works for NBC. Surprisingly, Oppenheim, NBC News' president, allowed Farrow to take his story to another media outlet.

Farrow acknowledges the culture of harassment at NBC which was broadly described by its numerous employees, targeting mostly women. Weinstein was aware of the numerous episodes of NBC executives' involvement in such practices. Two sources claimed that he threatened *Today*'s anchor, Matt Lauer with releasing leaked information. NBC's own harassing practices made them more susceptible to bribes and threats since they were used to hiding senior employee behaviors.

Despite numerous allegations that NBC's culture of harassment stemmed from Lack's behaviors, CEO Burke reinstated him. NBC then fired Lauer, Mark Halperin who was the news analyst and the senior vice president of booking, Matt Zimmerman.

A drop of courage in a pool of collusion, power, abuse, and money

Farrow considered taking his story to a different magazine, once Oppenheim used legal reasons why he and his colleague Rich McHugh should stop the investigations and interviews. He decided to go for *The New Yorker*. The in-house lawyer was surprised by NBC's desire to cease the investigation because of a fear of exposure, considering that this exposure can only happen once the story becomes public.

Nonetheless, *New Yorker*'s editor-in-chief David Remnick was the one who accepted Farrow's article. Considering the deep legal implications of Farrow's story, Remnick suggested reporting only the facts. Farrow recognizes this moment as one of relief, comparing it to *"those videos where lab animals walk on grass for the first time."*

The magazine's fact-checkers had to confirm his reporting before publishing. They considered whether "rape" was used correctly in this context. The story went live on October 10, 2017. The release of the story in media was shortly followed by calls from Weinstein's layers and numerous threatening letters. Farrow was impressed and was pleased with how many other women felt empowered to come further of more reports of Weinstein's abuse and sexual harassment.

Final thoughts

Nowadays, the truth can be easily hidden by money, power, and abuse. Farrow's work is a work-of-art that manages to shine despite the hardly digestible truths he shares with his readers. His interest is not prurient, however; the clear details of sexual assaults help the readers to understand how traumatizing Weinstein's victims were. Farrow pushed through the immense pressure in order to bring this story to light and he claims only one achievement: pursuing the good, old-fashioned reporting by chasing and exposing the truth.

Insights

In a reality governed by power, collusion, and abuse, Ronan Farrow manages to tell a story only whispered about. One of Hollywood's magnates is a predator and white sharks stick together. Follow Ronan Farrow's journey drawing closer to the truth!

An untold, unique story of exotic techniques of deep surveillance and intimidation, *Catch and Kill* relates how wealthy men work together to threaten journalists who expose the truths, along with the story of women who risked everything to fight back.

Breathtaking and fast-paced, Catch and Kill is a harrowing narration of journalist Ronan Farrow who fights with unseen resistance to uncover some of the wealthiest men's efforts to keep stories from publishing.

Meticulous and compulsively readable, 'Catch and Kill' recounts Ronan Farrow's investigation to reveal the harassing behaviors of Harvey Weinstein. Sharing hundreds of stories of abuse, he spotlights the emotional abuse of his victims, ending on a hopeful yet an almost tangible sense of disgust.

Catch and kill is an outrageous media technique of purchasing scandalous stories with the purpose of burying them and keeping influential people from being accused of their abuses. Countless people 'caught and killed' to protect Harvey Weinstein's women's abuse. Explore now a rich story about truth-telling and old-fashioned journalism!

Made in the USA
Las Vegas, NV
30 December 2020

15024070R00017